50 Beach BBQ Recipes for Home

By: Kelly Johnson

Table of Contents

- Grilled Lemon Garlic Shrimp Skewers
- Hawaiian Teriyaki Chicken Kebabs
- Citrus-Marinated Swordfish Steaks
- Coconut Lime Grilled Corn on the Cob
- Mango Jalapeno BBQ Ribs
- Grilled Pineapple Salsa
- Spicy Sriracha BBQ Wings
- Cajun Grilled Seafood Boil
- Grilled Lobster Tails with Garlic Butter
- Chili-Lime Grilled Avocado Halves
- Caribbean Jerk Pork Chops
- Chipotle Lime Grilled Chicken Thighs
- Grilled Veggie and Halloumi Skewers
- Tequila Lime Grilled Shrimp Tacos
- BBQ Bacon-Wrapped Scallops
- Pineapple Teriyaki Salmon Burgers
- Smoky BBQ Beef Brisket
- Grilled Caesar Salad with Parmesan Crisps
- Mango Chili Lime BBQ Drumsticks
- Coconut Rum Grilled Pineapple
- Mediterranean Grilled Vegetable Platter
- Thai Peanut Grilled Tofu Skewers
- Spicy Chipotle Grilled Corn Salad
- Grilled Octopus with Lemon and Garlic
- Jamaican Jerk Grilled Plantains
- Smoked Paprika BBQ Pork Ribs
- Grilled Clams with White Wine and Garlic
- Moroccan Spiced Grilled Lamb Chops
- Grilled Watermelon and Feta Salad
- Korean BBQ Beef Bulgogi
- BBQ Chicken and Pineapple Pizza
- Grilled Lobster Mac and Cheese
- Chili Lime Grilled Zucchini
- Honey Sriracha BBQ Wings
- Grilled Caesar Chicken Sandwiches

- Bourbon BBQ Glazed Pork Belly
- Mediterranean Grilled Swordfish
- Hawaiian BBQ Pork Sliders
- Grilled Portobello Mushrooms with Balsamic Glaze
- Chipotle BBQ Sweet Potato Wedges
- Tangy Mango BBQ Pulled Pork
- Grilled Asparagus with Lemon Zest
- BBQ Jackfruit Sandwiches
- Coconut Lime Grilled Sweet Potatoes
- Cajun Grilled Oysters
- Caribbean BBQ Chicken Quesadillas
- Grilled Eggplant Caprese Salad
- Smoked Salmon Dip with Grilled Pita
- Thai Chili Lime Grilled Beef Skewers
- BBQ Pineapple Upside-Down Cake

Grilled Lemon Garlic Shrimp Skewers

Ingredients:

- 1 pound large shrimp, peeled and deveined
- 3 cloves garlic, minced
- Zest of 1 lemon
- Juice of 1 lemon
- 2 tablespoons olive oil
- 1 tablespoon chopped fresh parsley
- Salt and black pepper, to taste
- Wooden or metal skewers

Instructions:

If using wooden skewers, soak them in water for about 30 minutes to prevent burning.

In a bowl, whisk together minced garlic, lemon zest, lemon juice, olive oil, chopped parsley, salt, and black pepper.

Add the peeled and deveined shrimp to the marinade, toss to coat evenly, and let it marinate in the refrigerator for 15-30 minutes.

Preheat the grill to medium-high heat.

Thread the marinated shrimp onto skewers, dividing them evenly.

Place the shrimp skewers on the preheated grill and cook for 2-3 minutes per side or until shrimp turn pink and opaque.

Remove from the grill and serve immediately as an appetizer or main dish.

Enjoy these delicious grilled lemon garlic shrimp skewers as a perfect beach BBQ treat!

Hawaiian Teriyaki Chicken Kebabs

Ingredients:

- 1.5 pounds boneless, skinless chicken thighs, cut into chunks
- 1 bell pepper, cut into chunks
- 1 red onion, cut into chunks
- 1 cup pineapple chunks (fresh or canned)
- Wooden or metal skewers

For the Teriyaki Marinade:

- 1/2 cup soy sauce
- 1/4 cup brown sugar
- 1/4 cup pineapple juice
- 2 tablespoons rice vinegar
- 2 cloves garlic, minced
- 1 teaspoon grated ginger
- 1 tablespoon cornstarch (optional, for thickening)

Instructions:

If using wooden skewers, soak them in water for about 30 minutes to prevent burning.
In a bowl, whisk together soy sauce, brown sugar, pineapple juice, rice vinegar, minced garlic, and grated ginger to make the teriyaki marinade.
Take about 1/2 cup of the marinade and set it aside for basting later.
Add the chicken chunks to the remaining marinade and toss to coat. Let it marinate in the refrigerator for at least 30 minutes (or up to 4 hours for best flavor).
Preheat your grill to medium-high heat.
Thread the marinated chicken onto skewers, alternating with bell pepper, red onion, and pineapple chunks.
Place the skewers on the preheated grill and cook for about 10-12 minutes, turning occasionally, or until the chicken is fully cooked and the vegetables are tender and lightly charred.
While grilling, baste the kebabs with the reserved marinade every few minutes.
Once cooked through, remove the kebabs from the grill and let them rest for a few minutes.
Serve the Hawaiian teriyaki chicken kebabs hot, garnished with chopped fresh cilantro or green onions if desired.

These flavorful teriyaki chicken kebabs with pineapple and veggies are a perfect addition to your beach BBQ menu!

Citrus-Marinated Swordfish Steaks

Ingredients:

- 4 swordfish steaks, about 6 ounces each
- Zest of 1 lemon
- Zest of 1 orange
- Juice of 1 lemon
- Juice of 1 orange
- 3 tablespoons olive oil
- 2 cloves garlic, minced
- 1 tablespoon chopped fresh parsley
- Salt and black pepper, to taste

Instructions:

In a bowl, whisk together the lemon zest, orange zest, lemon juice, orange juice, olive oil, minced garlic, chopped parsley, salt, and black pepper to create the citrus marinade.
Place the swordfish steaks in a shallow dish or a resealable plastic bag.
Pour the citrus marinade over the swordfish steaks, ensuring they are well coated. Cover or seal the dish/bag and refrigerate for at least 30 minutes to marinate (or up to 2 hours for more flavor).
Preheat your grill to medium-high heat.
Remove the swordfish steaks from the marinade and discard the remaining marinade. Place the swordfish steaks on the preheated grill and cook for about 4-5 minutes per side, or until the fish is cooked through and flakes easily with a fork. The internal temperature should reach 145°F (63°C).
While grilling, you can baste the swordfish with any leftover marinade to enhance the flavor.
Once cooked, remove the swordfish steaks from the grill and let them rest for a few minutes before serving.
Serve the citrus-marinated swordfish steaks hot, garnished with additional fresh parsley and lemon or orange wedges.

Enjoy these delicious and flavorful citrus-marinated swordfish steaks as a delightful beach BBQ dish!

Coconut Lime Grilled Corn on the Cob

Ingredients:

- 4 ears of corn, husked
- 1 can (14 ounces) coconut milk
- Zest and juice of 2 limes
- 2 tablespoons honey or maple syrup
- 2 tablespoons melted butter or coconut oil
- Salt and black pepper, to taste
- Chopped fresh cilantro (optional), for garnish

Instructions:

Preheat your grill to medium-high heat.
In a bowl, whisk together the coconut milk, lime zest, lime juice, honey or maple syrup, melted butter or coconut oil, salt, and black pepper to create the coconut lime marinade.
Place the husked ears of corn in a shallow dish or resealable plastic bag.
Pour the coconut lime marinade over the corn, ensuring they are well coated. Allow the corn to marinate for about 15-30 minutes.
Remove the corn from the marinade and reserve any leftover marinade for basting.
Place the corn directly on the preheated grill. Grill the corn for about 10-12 minutes, turning occasionally, until lightly charred and tender.
While grilling, brush the corn with the reserved marinade occasionally to enhance the flavor.
Once grilled to your liking, remove the corn from the grill and place them on a serving platter.
Garnish the coconut lime grilled corn with chopped fresh cilantro, if desired.
Serve the corn on the cob hot as a delightful and unique side dish for your beach BBQ.

This coconut lime grilled corn on the cob is a refreshing twist on a classic BBQ favorite, perfect for enjoying by the beach!

Mango Jalapeno BBQ Ribs

Ingredients:

- 2 racks of baby back ribs
- Salt and black pepper, to taste
- 1 cup mango puree (fresh or canned)
- 2 jalapeno peppers, seeded and finely chopped
- 1/2 cup ketchup
- 1/4 cup apple cider vinegar
- 2 tablespoons honey
- 2 cloves garlic, minced
- 1 teaspoon ground cumin
- 1/2 teaspoon smoked paprika
- 1/4 teaspoon cayenne pepper (optional, for heat)
- Fresh cilantro or parsley, chopped (for garnish)

Instructions:

Preheat your oven to 275°F (135°C).
Season the racks of baby back ribs with salt and black pepper.
Place the ribs on a large sheet of heavy-duty aluminum foil, and wrap tightly to form a packet. Place this packet on a baking sheet.
Bake the ribs in the preheated oven for 2.5 to 3 hours, or until the meat is tender and starts to pull away from the bones.
While the ribs are baking, prepare the mango jalapeno BBQ sauce. In a saucepan, combine the mango puree, chopped jalapeno peppers, ketchup, apple cider vinegar, honey, minced garlic, ground cumin, smoked paprika, and cayenne pepper (if using). Stir well to combine.
Bring the sauce to a simmer over medium heat, then reduce the heat to low. Let the sauce cook for about 15-20 minutes, stirring occasionally, until it thickens slightly.
Once the ribs are tender and cooked through, remove them from the oven and carefully unwrap the foil.
Heat your grill to medium-high heat.
Place the ribs on the grill and brush them generously with the mango jalapeno BBQ sauce.
Grill the ribs for about 5-7 minutes per side, brushing with additional sauce and turning occasionally, until the sauce caramelizes and the ribs are nicely glazed.

Remove the ribs from the grill and let them rest for a few minutes.
Cut the ribs into individual portions and garnish with chopped fresh cilantro or parsley.
Serve the mango jalapeno BBQ ribs hot and enjoy this flavorful and slightly spicy beach BBQ dish!

These mango jalapeno BBQ ribs are sure to be a hit at your next beach gathering, with a perfect blend of sweet, tangy, and spicy flavors.

Grilled Pineapple Salsa

Ingredients:

- 1 small pineapple, peeled and cored
- 1 red bell pepper, diced
- 1/2 red onion, finely chopped
- 1 jalapeno pepper, seeded and finely chopped
- Juice of 2 limes
- 1/4 cup chopped fresh cilantro
- Salt and pepper, to taste

Instructions:

Preheat your grill to medium-high heat.
Slice the pineapple into rings or spears.
Place the pineapple slices directly on the grill and grill for about 2-3 minutes per side, or until grill marks form and the pineapple begins to caramelize.
Remove the grilled pineapple from the grill and let it cool slightly. Dice the grilled pineapple into small pieces.
In a bowl, combine the diced grilled pineapple, diced red bell pepper, finely chopped red onion, and finely chopped jalapeno pepper.
Add the juice of 2 limes to the bowl and toss everything together.
Stir in the chopped fresh cilantro and season with salt and pepper to taste.
Mix well to combine all the ingredients.
Cover the bowl and refrigerate the grilled pineapple salsa for at least 30 minutes to allow the flavors to meld together.
Serve the grilled pineapple salsa chilled as a refreshing and flavorful topping for grilled meats, fish, tacos, or as a dip with tortilla chips.

This grilled pineapple salsa adds a delightful tropical twist to your beach BBQ menu and pairs beautifully with a variety of dishes. Enjoy the sweet and smoky flavors of this salsa at your next outdoor gathering!

Spicy Sriracha BBQ Wings

Ingredients:

- 2 pounds chicken wings, separated into flats and drumettes
- Salt and black pepper, to taste
- 1/2 cup Sriracha sauce
- 1/4 cup honey
- 2 tablespoons soy sauce
- 2 tablespoons rice vinegar
- 2 cloves garlic, minced
- 1 tablespoon grated ginger
- Sesame seeds, chopped green onions, and lime wedges for garnish (optional)

Instructions:

Preheat your grill to medium-high heat.
Season the chicken wings with salt and black pepper.
In a bowl, whisk together Sriracha sauce, honey, soy sauce, rice vinegar, minced garlic, and grated ginger to make the spicy Sriracha BBQ sauce.
Reserve about 1/4 cup of the sauce for basting later.
Place the chicken wings on the preheated grill and cook for about 10-12 minutes, turning occasionally, until they start to become crispy and golden brown.
Brush the wings with the reserved Sriracha BBQ sauce, turning and brushing occasionally, for an additional 2-3 minutes or until the wings are fully cooked and nicely glazed.
Remove the wings from the grill and transfer them to a serving platter.
Garnish the spicy Sriracha BBQ wings with sesame seeds, chopped green onions, and lime wedges if desired.
Serve the wings hot as a deliciously spicy appetizer or main dish for your beach BBQ.

These spicy Sriracha BBQ wings are packed with flavor and heat, making them a crowd-pleaser at any outdoor gathering. Enjoy the sweet and spicy combination of this finger-licking dish!

Cajun Grilled Seafood Boil

Ingredients:

- 1 pound large shrimp, peeled and deveined
- 1 pound mussels, cleaned and debearded
- 1 pound clams, scrubbed
- 1 pound baby potatoes, halved
- 2 ears of corn, shucked and cut into thirds
- 1 onion, cut into wedges
- 1 lemon, cut into wedges
- Cajun seasoning (store-bought or homemade)
- Salt, to taste
- Butter, for serving

For the Cajun Seasoning:

- 2 tablespoons paprika
- 1 tablespoon garlic powder
- 1 tablespoon onion powder
- 1 tablespoon dried oregano
- 1 tablespoon dried thyme
- 1 tablespoon cayenne pepper (adjust to taste)
- Salt and black pepper, to taste

Instructions:

Preheat your grill to medium-high heat.
In a bowl, mix together all the ingredients for the Cajun seasoning.
In a large pot of boiling water, parboil the baby potatoes for about 8-10 minutes until slightly tender. Drain and set aside.
Season the shrimp, mussels, clams, corn, onion wedges, and lemon wedges with the Cajun seasoning and a pinch of salt.
Thread the seasoned shrimp, mussels, clams, corn, onion, and lemon onto skewers, or use a grill basket for easier grilling.
Place the skewers or grill basket on the preheated grill and cook for about 5-7 minutes, turning occasionally, until the seafood is cooked through and the vegetables are tender and lightly charred.

While grilling, brush the seafood and vegetables with melted butter for extra flavor.

Remove the grilled seafood boil components from the grill and transfer them to a large serving platter or bowl.

Serve the Cajun grilled seafood boil hot, sprinkled with additional Cajun seasoning if desired, and accompanied by melted butter for dipping.

This Cajun grilled seafood boil is a festive and flavorful dish that's perfect for a beach BBQ, combining the bold flavors of Cajun spices with fresh seafood and vegetables grilled to perfection. Enjoy this mouthwatering seafood feast with family and friends!

Grilled Lobster Tails with Garlic Butter

Ingredients:

- 4 lobster tails
- Salt and black pepper, to taste
- 1/2 cup unsalted butter, melted
- 3 cloves garlic, minced
- Juice of 1 lemon
- 2 tablespoons chopped fresh parsley
- Lemon wedges, for serving

Instructions:

Preheat your grill to medium-high heat.
Use kitchen shears to cut the top of each lobster tail shell lengthwise, stopping at the tail. Gently pry the shell open and lift the lobster meat, leaving it attached at the base of the tail.
Season the lobster tails with salt and black pepper.
In a small bowl, combine melted butter, minced garlic, lemon juice, and chopped parsley to make the garlic butter sauce.
Brush the garlic butter sauce generously over the exposed lobster meat.
Place the lobster tails on the preheated grill, shell side down. Close the grill lid and cook for about 8-10 minutes, or until the lobster meat is opaque and lightly charred, and the shells turn bright red.
Occasionally brush the lobster tails with more garlic butter sauce while grilling.
Carefully remove the grilled lobster tails from the grill and transfer them to a serving platter.
Serve the grilled lobster tails hot, garnished with additional chopped parsley and lemon wedges on the side.

These grilled lobster tails with garlic butter are a luxurious and impressive dish for your beach BBQ, showcasing the natural sweetness of lobster complemented by savory garlic butter. Enjoy this delightful seafood treat with family and friends!

Chili-Lime Grilled Avocado Halves

Ingredients:

- 2 ripe avocados
- Juice of 1 lime
- 1 tablespoon olive oil
- 1 teaspoon chili powder
- 1/2 teaspoon ground cumin
- Salt and black pepper, to taste
- Fresh cilantro, chopped (for garnish)

Instructions:

Preheat your grill to medium-high heat.
Cut the avocados in half and remove the pits. Leave the skin on.
In a bowl, whisk together lime juice, olive oil, chili powder, ground cumin, salt, and black pepper.
Brush the cut side of each avocado half with the chili-lime mixture.
Place the avocado halves, cut side down, on the preheated grill.
Grill the avocados for about 3-4 minutes, until grill marks appear and the avocados start to soften slightly.
Carefully remove the grilled avocado halves from the grill and transfer them to a serving platter.
Drizzle any remaining chili-lime mixture over the grilled avocados.
Garnish with chopped fresh cilantro.
Serve the chili-lime grilled avocado halves hot as a tasty and healthy side dish or appetizer for your beach BBQ.

These chili-lime grilled avocado halves are creamy, smoky, and packed with flavor, making them a unique and delicious addition to your outdoor barbecue menu. Enjoy the bold flavors and beautiful presentation of this dish!

Caribbean Jerk Pork Chops

Ingredients:

- 4 bone-in pork chops, about 1-inch thick
- Salt and black pepper, to taste
- 3 tablespoons Caribbean jerk seasoning (store-bought or homemade)
- 2 tablespoons olive oil
- Juice of 1 lime
- 2 tablespoons soy sauce
- 2 tablespoons honey
- 2 cloves garlic, minced
- 1 tablespoon grated fresh ginger
- Chopped fresh cilantro or parsley, for garnish

Instructions:

Season the pork chops generously with salt and black pepper on both sides.
Rub the Caribbean jerk seasoning all over the pork chops, coating them evenly. Let them marinate for at least 30 minutes (or longer for more flavor) in the refrigerator.
In a bowl, whisk together olive oil, lime juice, soy sauce, honey, minced garlic, and grated ginger to make the marinade.
Place the seasoned pork chops in a shallow dish or resealable plastic bag. Pour the marinade over the pork chops, ensuring they are well coated. Cover or seal the dish/bag and refrigerate for at least 1 hour (or up to overnight).
Preheat your grill to medium-high heat.
Remove the pork chops from the marinade, allowing any excess marinade to drip off.
Grill the pork chops for about 4-5 minutes per side, or until they reach an internal temperature of 145°F (63°C) and are nicely charred and cooked through.
Remove the pork chops from the grill and let them rest for a few minutes.
Sprinkle chopped fresh cilantro or parsley over the grilled Caribbean jerk pork chops for garnish.
Serve the pork chops hot with your favorite side dishes, such as rice, beans, grilled vegetables, or a tropical salad.

These Caribbean jerk pork chops are bursting with spicy, sweet, and tangy flavors, making them a fantastic choice for a beach BBQ. Enjoy the taste of the Caribbean with this delicious grilled pork dish!

Chipotle Lime Grilled Chicken Thighs

Ingredients:

- 8 boneless, skinless chicken thighs
- Salt and black pepper, to taste
- 2 chipotle peppers in adobo sauce, finely chopped
- Zest and juice of 2 limes
- 3 tablespoons olive oil
- 2 tablespoons honey
- 2 cloves garlic, minced
- 1 teaspoon ground cumin
- Chopped fresh cilantro, for garnish

Instructions:

Season the chicken thighs with salt and black pepper on both sides.
In a bowl, combine the finely chopped chipotle peppers, lime zest, lime juice, olive oil, honey, minced garlic, and ground cumin to make the marinade.
Place the chicken thighs in a shallow dish or resealable plastic bag. Pour the marinade over the chicken, making sure each thigh is well coated. Cover or seal the dish/bag and refrigerate for at least 30 minutes (or up to 4 hours for more flavor).
Preheat your grill to medium-high heat.
Remove the chicken thighs from the marinade, allowing any excess marinade to drip off.
Grill the chicken thighs for about 6-8 minutes per side, or until they are cooked through and have nice grill marks.
While grilling, brush the chicken thighs with any remaining marinade to enhance the flavor.
Once cooked through, remove the chicken thighs from the grill and let them rest for a few minutes.
Garnish the chipotle lime grilled chicken thighs with chopped fresh cilantro.
Serve the chicken thighs hot with rice, quinoa, salad, or your favorite side dishes.

These chipotle lime grilled chicken thighs are packed with smoky, spicy, and tangy flavors, making them a delicious and satisfying main dish for your beach BBQ. Enjoy the zesty kick of lime and chipotle with juicy grilled chicken thighs!

Grilled Veggie and Halloumi Skewers

Ingredients:

- 1 block of halloumi cheese, cut into cubes
- 1 red bell pepper, cut into chunks
- 1 yellow bell pepper, cut into chunks
- 1 zucchini, sliced into rounds
- 1 red onion, cut into chunks
- Cherry tomatoes
- Wooden or metal skewers

For the Marinade:

- 1/4 cup olive oil
- Juice of 1 lemon
- 2 cloves garlic, minced
- 1 tablespoon fresh herbs (such as thyme, rosemary, or oregano), chopped
- Salt and black pepper, to taste

Instructions:

If using wooden skewers, soak them in water for about 30 minutes to prevent burning.
In a bowl, whisk together the olive oil, lemon juice, minced garlic, chopped herbs, salt, and black pepper to make the marinade.
Assemble the skewers by threading alternating pieces of halloumi cheese, bell peppers, zucchini slices, red onion chunks, and cherry tomatoes onto the skewers.
Place the assembled skewers in a shallow dish and brush them generously with the marinade, making sure to coat all sides.
Let the skewers marinate in the refrigerator for at least 30 minutes (or longer for more flavor).
Preheat your grill to medium-high heat.
Grill the veggie and halloumi skewers for about 5-7 minutes per side, or until the vegetables are tender and slightly charred, and the halloumi cheese is golden brown and has grill marks.
While grilling, you can brush the skewers with any leftover marinade for added flavor.
Once grilled to perfection, remove the skewers from the grill and transfer them to a serving platter.
Serve the grilled veggie and halloumi skewers hot as a delightful vegetarian option for your beach BBQ.

These grilled veggie and halloumi skewers are colorful, flavorful, and make a fantastic addition to any outdoor gathering. Enjoy the combination of grilled vegetables and savory halloumi cheese in every bite!

Tequila Lime Grilled Shrimp Tacos

Ingredients:

For the Tequila Lime Marinade:

- 1/4 cup tequila
- Juice of 2 limes
- 2 tablespoons olive oil
- 2 cloves garlic, minced
- 1 teaspoon chili powder
- 1 teaspoon cumin
- Salt and pepper, to taste

For the Shrimp Tacos:

- 1 pound large shrimp, peeled and deveined
- Corn or flour tortillas
- Shredded cabbage or lettuce
- Diced tomatoes
- Sliced avocado
- Chopped cilantro, for garnish
- Lime wedges, for serving

Instructions:

In a bowl, whisk together the tequila, lime juice, olive oil, minced garlic, chili powder, cumin, salt, and pepper to create the marinade.
Place the peeled and deveined shrimp in a shallow dish or resealable plastic bag. Pour the marinade over the shrimp, making sure they are well coated. Marinate in the refrigerator for at least 30 minutes (or up to 2 hours) to allow the flavors to meld.
Preheat your grill to medium-high heat.
Thread the marinated shrimp onto skewers for easier grilling.
Grill the shrimp skewers for about 2-3 minutes per side, or until the shrimp are pink and opaque.
While the shrimp are grilling, warm the tortillas on the grill for about 30 seconds on each side, or until they are lightly toasted and pliable.
Assemble the shrimp tacos by placing a layer of shredded cabbage or lettuce on each tortilla.

Top with grilled shrimp, diced tomatoes, sliced avocado, and chopped cilantro. Squeeze fresh lime juice over the tacos and serve immediately.

Enjoy these delicious tequila lime grilled shrimp tacos as a flavorful and satisfying dish for your beach BBQ! Adjust the toppings and seasonings according to your preferences for a perfect taco experience.

BBQ Bacon-Wrapped Scallops

Ingredients:

- 12 large sea scallops
- 6 slices of bacon, cut in half crosswise
- BBQ sauce (your favorite store-bought or homemade)
- Salt and black pepper, to taste
- Toothpicks or skewers (if using wooden, soak in water)

Instructions:

Prepare the Scallops:
- Rinse the scallops under cold water and pat them dry with paper towels.
- Season the scallops lightly with salt and black pepper.

Wrap the Scallops with Bacon:
- Take each scallop and wrap it with a half-slice of bacon, securing the bacon with a toothpick through the sides to hold it in place. Repeat for all scallops.

Preheat the Grill:
- Preheat your grill to medium-high heat (about 375-400°F or 190-200°C).

Grill the Bacon-Wrapped Scallops:
- Place the bacon-wrapped scallops directly on the preheated grill grate.
- Grill the scallops for about 3-4 minutes per side, or until the bacon is crispy and the scallops are cooked through. Rotate the scallops halfway through cooking to ensure even grilling.

Brush with BBQ Sauce:
- During the last few minutes of grilling, brush each scallop generously with BBQ sauce on all sides.
- Continue grilling for another minute or so after saucing, allowing the sauce to caramelize slightly.

Serve:
- Carefully remove the BBQ bacon-wrapped scallops from the grill.
- Discard the toothpicks before serving.

Garnish and Enjoy:
- Transfer the grilled scallops to a serving platter.
- Garnish with chopped fresh parsley or chives for a pop of color and flavor.
- Serve the BBQ bacon-wrapped scallops hot as an appetizer or main dish.

Note:

- Make sure to monitor the grill closely to prevent burning the bacon. Adjust the heat as needed.

- Serve the BBQ bacon-wrapped scallops with additional BBQ sauce on the side for dipping, if desired.
- These scallops are perfect for summer gatherings and will surely be a hit at your beach BBQ! Adjust seasoning and sauce according to your taste preferences. Enjoy!

Pineapple Teriyaki Salmon Burgers

Ingredients:

- 1 pound fresh salmon fillets, skin removed
- 1 cup finely chopped pineapple (fresh or canned)
- 2 green onions, finely chopped
- 1 tablespoon soy sauce
- 1 tablespoon hoisin sauce
- 1 tablespoon fresh lime juice
- 1 tablespoon honey
- 1 teaspoon grated fresh ginger
- 1 clove garlic, minced
- Salt and pepper, to taste
- 4 burger buns
- Lettuce leaves, for serving
- Sliced tomato, for serving
- Sliced red onion, for serving
- Mayonnaise or teriyaki sauce, for topping (optional)

Instructions:

Prepare the Salmon Patties:
- Cut the salmon fillets into small pieces and place them in a food processor.
- Pulse a few times until the salmon is finely chopped but still has some texture.
- Transfer the chopped salmon to a mixing bowl.

Make the Burger Mixture:
- To the bowl with the chopped salmon, add the finely chopped pineapple, green onions, soy sauce, hoisin sauce, lime juice, honey, grated ginger, minced garlic, salt, and pepper.
- Mix everything together until well combined. The mixture should hold together when shaped into patties.

Form and Cook the Salmon Burgers:
- Divide the salmon mixture into 4 equal portions.
- Shape each portion into a patty of desired thickness, using your hands.
- Preheat a grill or skillet over medium-high heat.
- Brush the grill or skillet with a little oil to prevent sticking.
- Cook the salmon patties for about 4-5 minutes per side, or until cooked through and nicely browned on the outside.

Assemble the Burgers:
- Toast the burger buns lightly on the grill or in a toaster.
- Spread mayonnaise or teriyaki sauce on the bottom halves of the burger buns (optional).

- Place a salmon patty on each bottom bun.
- Top with lettuce leaves, sliced tomato, and sliced red onion.

Serve and Enjoy:
- Place the top halves of the burger buns over the toppings to complete the burgers.
- Serve the pineapple teriyaki salmon burgers immediately.
- Optionally, serve with additional teriyaki sauce on the side for dipping or drizzling.
- Enjoy these delicious and flavorful salmon burgers with a tropical twist!

Note:

- You can customize the toppings and condiments based on your preferences.
- These pineapple teriyaki salmon burgers are great for a summer beach BBQ, offering a delightful combination of sweet pineapple and savory salmon flavors. Adjust the seasonings and sauces to suit your taste.

Smoky BBQ Beef Brisket

Ingredients:

- 1 beef brisket, about 4-5 pounds
- Salt and black pepper, to taste
- 2 tablespoons smoked paprika
- 1 tablespoon garlic powder
- 1 tablespoon onion powder
- 1 tablespoon brown sugar
- 1 teaspoon cayenne pepper (adjust to taste)
- 1 cup BBQ sauce (your favorite store-bought or homemade)
- 1/2 cup beef broth or water
- Wood chips (for smoking, optional)

Instructions:

Preheat the Smoker (or Oven):
- If using a smoker, preheat it to 225-250°F (110-120°C) according to manufacturer's instructions. If using an oven, preheat it to 250°F (120°C).

Prepare the Brisket:
- Trim any excess fat from the surface of the brisket, leaving a thin layer for flavor and moisture.
- Season the brisket generously with salt and black pepper on all sides.

Make the Dry Rub:
- In a small bowl, mix together the smoked paprika, garlic powder, onion powder, brown sugar, and cayenne pepper to create the dry rub.
- Rub the dry rub mixture all over the seasoned brisket, ensuring even coverage.

Smoke (or Roast) the Brisket:
- If using a smoker, place the brisket directly on the smoker rack.
- If using an oven, place the brisket in a roasting pan or on a rack inside a baking dish.
- Optional: Add soaked wood chips to the smoker box or wrap in foil for additional smoky flavor.
- Smoke or roast the brisket low and slow for several hours, allowing it to cook until tender. Plan for approximately 1.5 to 2 hours per pound of brisket.

Baste with BBQ Sauce:
- After the brisket has been cooking for a few hours (usually around the halfway mark), mix together the BBQ sauce and beef broth (or water) in a bowl.
- Baste the brisket with the BBQ sauce mixture, brushing it over the surface.
- Continue cooking until the internal temperature of the brisket reaches about 195-205°F (90-95°C) and the meat is tender and easily pierced with a fork.

Rest and Serve:

- Once cooked to perfection, remove the brisket from the smoker or oven.
- Let the brisket rest for at least 30 minutes before slicing to allow the juices to redistribute.
- Slice the brisket against the grain into thick slices.
- Serve the smoky BBQ beef brisket with additional BBQ sauce on the side, if desired.

Tips:

- For extra smoky flavor, use wood chips like hickory, oak, or mesquite in your smoker.
- Maintain a consistent cooking temperature throughout the smoking or roasting process for the best results.
- Brisket is done when it is fork-tender and easily pulls apart. Cooking times can vary based on the size and thickness of the brisket.
- Enjoy this smoky BBQ beef brisket as a main dish at your beach BBQ, served with classic sides like coleslaw, baked beans, cornbread, or potato salad.

Grilled Caesar Salad with Parmesan Crisps

Ingredients:

For the Caesar Salad:

- Romaine lettuce hearts, halved lengthwise
- Olive oil
- Salt and black pepper, to taste
- Caesar dressing (store-bought or homemade)
- Grated Parmesan cheese, for garnish

For the Parmesan Crisps:

- 1 cup grated Parmesan cheese

Instructions:

Prepare the Parmesan Crisps:
- Preheat your grill to medium-high heat.
- Line a baking sheet with parchment paper.
- Sprinkle grated Parmesan cheese in small mounds (about 1 tablespoon each) on the prepared baking sheet, leaving space between each mound.
- Place the baking sheet on the grill and close the lid.
- Grill the Parmesan mounds for 3-4 minutes, or until the cheese is melted, bubbly, and golden brown.
- Remove the baking sheet from the grill and let the Parmesan crisps cool and harden. Set aside.

Grill the Romaine Lettuce:
- Brush the halved romaine lettuce hearts with olive oil on both sides.
- Season with salt and black pepper.
- Place the lettuce halves directly on the preheated grill, cut side down.
- Grill for 2-3 minutes, or until grill marks appear and the lettuce starts to wilt slightly.
- Remove the grilled lettuce from the grill and transfer to a serving platter.

Assemble the Grilled Caesar Salad:
- Drizzle Caesar dressing over the grilled romaine lettuce.
- Sprinkle with grated Parmesan cheese.
- Place the Parmesan crisps on top of the salad for a crunchy texture and additional flavor.

Serve and Enjoy:
- Serve the grilled Caesar salad immediately while the lettuce is still warm from the grill.
- Enjoy this unique and delicious twist on a classic Caesar salad with grilled flavors and crispy Parmesan toppings.

Notes:

- You can customize this grilled Caesar salad by adding grilled chicken, shrimp, or other protein of your choice.
- Feel free to use your favorite Caesar dressing or make a homemade version with anchovies, garlic, lemon juice, Dijon mustard, Parmesan cheese, and olive oil.
- This salad makes a great appetizer or side dish for any summer gathering or beach BBQ, offering a delightful combination of smoky, grilled flavors with a classic Caesar salad base.

Mango Chili Lime BBQ Drumsticks

Ingredients:

- 8-10 chicken drumsticks
- 1 ripe mango, peeled and diced
- 2 tablespoons chili powder
- Zest and juice of 2 limes
- 3 tablespoons honey
- 2 tablespoons soy sauce
- 2 cloves garlic, minced
- Salt and black pepper, to taste
- Chopped fresh cilantro, for garnish (optional)
- Lime wedges, for serving

Instructions:

Prepare the Mango Chili Lime BBQ Sauce:
- In a blender or food processor, combine the diced mango, chili powder, lime zest, lime juice, honey, soy sauce, minced garlic, salt, and black pepper.
- Blend until smooth and well combined. Adjust seasoning to taste.

Marinate the Drumsticks:
- Place the chicken drumsticks in a large bowl or resealable plastic bag.
- Pour the mango chili lime BBQ sauce over the drumsticks, reserving some sauce for basting and serving.
- Massage the sauce into the drumsticks to ensure they are well coated.
- Cover the bowl or seal the bag, and refrigerate for at least 1 hour (or overnight) to marinate.

Preheat the Grill:
- Preheat your grill to medium-high heat.

Grill the Drumsticks:
- Remove the drumsticks from the marinade, allowing any excess marinade to drip off.
- Place the drumsticks on the preheated grill and cook for about 20-25 minutes, turning occasionally, until the chicken is cooked through and nicely charred.
- During the last few minutes of grilling, brush the drumsticks with the reserved mango chili lime BBQ sauce, turning and basting to glaze the chicken.

Serve:
- Remove the grilled drumsticks from the grill and transfer them to a serving platter.
- Garnish with chopped fresh cilantro, if desired.
- Serve the mango chili lime BBQ drumsticks hot, accompanied by lime wedges for squeezing over the chicken.

Notes:

- Adjust the amount of chili powder based on your spice preference. You can increase or decrease the heat level by adding more or less chili powder.
- Make sure the chicken drumsticks reach an internal temperature of 165°F (75°C) before serving.
- This recipe pairs well with rice, quinoa, or a fresh salad. Enjoy these flavorful mango chili lime BBQ drumsticks at your next beach BBQ or summer gathering!

Coconut Rum Grilled Pineapple

Ingredients:

- 1 ripe pineapple, peeled, cored, and sliced into rings or wedges
- 1/2 cup coconut rum
- 1/4 cup brown sugar
- 1/4 cup melted butter
- Pinch of salt
- Optional: Vanilla ice cream or whipped cream, for serving
- Fresh mint leaves, for garnish

Instructions:

Prepare the Pineapple:
- Slice the pineapple into rings or wedges, removing the tough core.

Marinate the Pineapple:
- In a bowl, combine the coconut rum, brown sugar, melted butter, and a pinch of salt.
- Whisk together until the sugar is dissolved.
- Place the pineapple slices in a shallow dish or resealable plastic bag.
- Pour the marinade over the pineapple slices, ensuring they are well coated.
- Let the pineapple marinate for at least 30 minutes, turning occasionally to coat evenly.

Preheat the Grill:
- Preheat your grill to medium-high heat.

Grill the Pineapple:
- Remove the pineapple slices from the marinade and shake off any excess.
- Place the pineapple slices directly on the preheated grill.
- Grill for 3-4 minutes per side, or until caramelized and grill marks appear.
- During grilling, brush the pineapple slices with any remaining marinade for extra flavor.

Serve:
- Remove the grilled pineapple from the grill and transfer to a serving platter.
- Serve the coconut rum grilled pineapple hot or warm.
- Optionally, serve with a scoop of vanilla ice cream or a dollop of whipped cream on top.
- Garnish with fresh mint leaves for a pop of color and freshness.

Notes:

- You can adjust the sweetness by adding more or less brown sugar to the marinade.

- Make sure to watch the pineapple closely while grilling to prevent burning.
- Enjoy this delicious coconut rum grilled pineapple as a refreshing and tropical dessert at your beach BBQ or summer party!

Mediterranean Grilled Vegetable Platter

Ingredients:

- 2 zucchini, sliced lengthwise
- 2 yellow squash, sliced lengthwise
- 1 large eggplant, sliced into rounds
- 2 bell peppers (red, yellow, or orange), seeded and quartered
- 1 red onion, sliced into thick rounds
- 1 pint cherry tomatoes
- 1/4 cup extra-virgin olive oil
- 3 cloves garlic, minced
- 1 tablespoon balsamic vinegar
- 1 tablespoon chopped fresh herbs (such as basil, oregano, or thyme)
- Salt and black pepper, to taste
- Lemon wedges, for serving
- Crumbled feta cheese (optional), for garnish

Instructions:

Preheat the Grill:
- Preheat your grill to medium-high heat.

Prepare the Vegetables:
- In a large bowl, toss the sliced zucchini, yellow squash, eggplant, bell peppers, red onion, and cherry tomatoes with olive oil, minced garlic, balsamic vinegar, chopped fresh herbs, salt, and black pepper.
- Make sure all the vegetables are coated evenly with the marinade.

Grill the Vegetables:
- Place the vegetables on the preheated grill in a single layer.
- Grill the vegetables for 3-4 minutes per side, or until tender and charred.
- Remove each vegetable from the grill as it finishes cooking and transfer to a serving platter.

Assemble the Grilled Vegetable Platter:
- Arrange the grilled vegetables on a large serving platter.
- Drizzle any remaining marinade over the vegetables.
- Sprinkle with crumbled feta cheese, if using.

Serve:
- Serve the Mediterranean grilled vegetable platter warm or at room temperature.
- Garnish with additional chopped fresh herbs and lemon wedges on the side.
- Enjoy as a delicious and colorful side dish or appetizer for your beach BBQ or outdoor gathering.

Notes:

- Feel free to customize the selection of vegetables based on what's in season and your preferences.
- You can add other Mediterranean-inspired ingredients such as olives, capers, or sun-dried tomatoes to enhance the flavors.
- This grilled vegetable platter pairs well with grilled meats, fish, or a selection of dips like hummus or tzatziki.
- Enjoy the vibrant and flavorful taste of Mediterranean cuisine with this easy and healthy grilled vegetable platter!

Thai Peanut Grilled Tofu Skewers

Ingredients:

- 1 block (14-16 oz) extra-firm tofu, pressed and cut into cubes
- 1 red bell pepper, cut into chunks
- 1 yellow bell pepper, cut into chunks
- 1 zucchini, sliced into rounds
- Wooden skewers, soaked in water for 30 minutes

For the Thai Peanut Marinade:

- 1/4 cup creamy peanut butter
- 2 tablespoons soy sauce (or tamari for gluten-free)
- 2 tablespoons lime juice
- 2 tablespoons water
- 1 tablespoon maple syrup or honey
- 1 tablespoon sriracha sauce (adjust to taste)
- 2 cloves garlic, minced
- 1 teaspoon grated ginger
- Chopped fresh cilantro, for garnish
- Crushed peanuts, for garnish (optional)

Instructions:

Prepare the Tofu:
- Press the tofu to remove excess water. Slice the tofu into cubes of desired size.

Make the Thai Peanut Marinade:
- In a bowl, whisk together peanut butter, soy sauce, lime juice, water, maple syrup (or honey), sriracha sauce, minced garlic, and grated ginger until smooth and well combined.

Marinate the Tofu and Vegetables:
- Place the tofu cubes and vegetable chunks in a shallow dish or large resealable plastic bag.
- Pour the Thai peanut marinade over the tofu and vegetables, reserving a portion for brushing later.
- Toss gently to coat the tofu and vegetables evenly with the marinade.
- Cover and refrigerate for at least 30 minutes to allow the flavors to meld.

Assemble the Skewers:
- Preheat your grill to medium-high heat.
- Thread the marinated tofu cubes and vegetables onto the soaked wooden skewers, alternating between tofu and vegetables.

Grill the Skewers:
- Place the assembled skewers on the preheated grill.
- Grill for about 8-10 minutes, turning occasionally, until the tofu is nicely charred and the vegetables are tender-crisp.

Serve:
- Remove the grilled Thai peanut tofu skewers from the grill.
- Brush with the reserved marinade.
- Garnish with chopped fresh cilantro and crushed peanuts, if desired.

Enjoy:
- Serve the Thai peanut grilled tofu skewers hot as a delicious and flavorful main dish or appetizer.
- Pair with steamed rice or noodles and extra peanut sauce on the side for dipping.

Notes:

- Customize the vegetables based on your preferences. You can also use mushrooms, cherry tomatoes, or onion wedges.
- Adjust the level of spiciness by adding more or less sriracha sauce.
- This recipe is vegan and gluten-free (if using tamari instead of soy sauce). It's packed with Thai-inspired flavors and perfect for your beach BBQ or outdoor gathering!

Spicy Chipotle Grilled Corn Salad

Ingredients:

- 4 ears of corn, husked
- 1 red bell pepper, diced
- 1/2 red onion, finely diced
- 1 jalapeño pepper, seeded and finely chopped
- 1/4 cup chopped fresh cilantro
- 1 avocado, diced
- Juice of 1 lime
- 2 tablespoons olive oil
- 1-2 chipotle peppers in adobo sauce, finely chopped (adjust to taste)
- 1 teaspoon ground cumin
- Salt and pepper, to taste
- Optional: Crumbled cotija cheese or feta cheese for garnish

Instructions:

Grill the Corn:
- Preheat your grill to medium-high heat.
- Place the husked ears of corn directly on the grill.
- Grill the corn for about 10-12 minutes, turning occasionally, until kernels are charred and tender.
- Remove from the grill and let cool slightly.

Prepare the Salad:
- Once the corn is cool enough to handle, use a sharp knife to carefully cut the kernels off the cobs into a large mixing bowl.

Assemble the Salad:
- Add the diced red bell pepper, finely diced red onion, chopped jalapeño pepper, chopped cilantro, and diced avocado to the bowl with the grilled corn.

Make the Dressing:
- In a small bowl, whisk together the lime juice, olive oil, finely chopped chipotle peppers in adobo sauce, ground cumin, salt, and pepper.

Combine and Toss:
- Pour the dressing over the salad ingredients in the bowl.
- Gently toss everything together until well combined and evenly coated with the dressing.

Chill (Optional):
- For best flavor, cover the salad and refrigerate for at least 30 minutes to allow the flavors to meld together.

Serve:
- Before serving, taste and adjust seasoning if needed.

- Garnish with crumbled cotija cheese or feta cheese, if desired.
- Serve the spicy chipotle grilled corn salad as a side dish or appetizer at your beach BBQ or outdoor gathering.

Notes:

- Adjust the spiciness of the salad by adding more or less chipotle peppers in adobo sauce.
- You can substitute cotija cheese with feta cheese or omit it for a vegan option.
- This salad is best served fresh but can be refrigerated for a few hours before serving.
- Enjoy the bold flavors and smoky goodness of this spicy chipotle grilled corn salad!

Grilled Octopus with Lemon and Garlic

Ingredients:

- 1 whole octopus (about 2-3 pounds), cleaned and thawed if frozen
- 4-5 cloves garlic, minced
- Zest and juice of 2 lemons
- 1/4 cup extra-virgin olive oil
- Salt and black pepper, to taste
- Chopped fresh parsley, for garnish
- Lemon wedges, for serving

Instructions:

Prep the Octopus:
- If using a fresh octopus, clean it thoroughly by removing the beak, eyes, and innards.
- Rinse the octopus under cold water and pat dry with paper towels.

Tenderize the Octopus (Optional):

To tenderize the octopus, you can either:

a) Freeze it overnight and thaw before cooking, or

- b) Use a meat mallet or the back of a knife to gently pound the octopus before cooking.

Marinate the Octopus:
- In a bowl, whisk together minced garlic, lemon zest, lemon juice, olive oil, salt, and black pepper to create the marinade.
- Place the cleaned octopus in a shallow dish or resealable plastic bag.
- Pour the marinade over the octopus, making sure it's evenly coated.
- Cover and refrigerate for at least 1-2 hours to marinate.

Preheat the Grill:
- Preheat your grill to medium-high heat.

Grill the Octopus:
- Remove the marinated octopus from the refrigerator.
- Shake off any excess marinade and discard the marinade.
- Place the octopus directly on the preheated grill.
- Grill the octopus for about 3-4 minutes per side, or until charred and cooked through.
- Octopus is cooked when it turns opaque and firms up slightly.

Serve:
- Remove the grilled octopus from the grill and transfer to a serving platter.

- Drizzle with a little extra olive oil and sprinkle with chopped fresh parsley.
- Serve hot with lemon wedges on the side.

Tips:

- Be careful not to overcook the octopus, as it can become tough and rubbery.
- You can also add additional seasonings or spices to the marinade, such as crushed red pepper flakes or dried oregano, for extra flavor.
- Grilled octopus makes a wonderful appetizer or main course for a beach BBQ or special occasion. Enjoy the delicious flavors of lemon and garlic with perfectly grilled octopus!

Jamaican Jerk Grilled Plantains

Ingredients:

- 2 ripe plantains, peeled and sliced diagonally into 1-inch thick pieces
- 2 tablespoons Jamaican jerk seasoning (store-bought or homemade)
- 2 tablespoons olive oil or melted coconut oil
- Juice of 1 lime
- Salt, to taste
- Fresh cilantro or parsley, chopped (for garnish, optional)

Instructions:

Prepare the Plantains:
- Peel the plantains and slice them diagonally into 1-inch thick pieces.

Marinate the Plantains:
- In a bowl, combine the sliced plantains with Jamaican jerk seasoning, olive oil (or melted coconut oil), lime juice, and a pinch of salt.
- Toss the plantains gently to coat them evenly with the marinade.

Grill the Plantains:
- Preheat your grill to medium-high heat.
- Place the marinated plantain slices directly on the grill grates.
- Grill the plantains for about 3-4 minutes per side, or until they are caramelized and have grill marks.

Serve:
- Remove the grilled plantains from the grill and transfer them to a serving platter.
- Sprinkle with chopped fresh cilantro or parsley for garnish, if desired.
- Serve the Jamaican jerk grilled plantains hot as a side dish or appetizer.

Tips:

- Make sure to use ripe plantains for this recipe, as they will be sweeter and more flavorful when grilled.
- If you prefer spicier plantains, you can increase the amount of Jamaican jerk seasoning or add a dash of cayenne pepper to the marinade.
- Serve these delicious grilled plantains alongside grilled meats, seafood, or as part of a tropical-themed meal.
- Enjoy the sweet and savory flavors of Jamaican jerk grilled plantains at your next beach BBQ or summer gathering!

Smoked Paprika BBQ Pork Ribs

Ingredients:

- 2 racks of pork ribs (about 4-5 pounds total)
- 2 tablespoons smoked paprika
- 1 tablespoon brown sugar
- 1 tablespoon garlic powder
- 1 tablespoon onion powder
- 1 tablespoon salt
- 1 teaspoon black pepper
- 1 cup BBQ sauce (your favorite store-bought or homemade)
- Wood chips for smoking (applewood, hickory, or your choice)

Instructions:

Prepare the Ribs:
- Remove the membrane from the back of the ribs by sliding a knife under the membrane and then using a paper towel to grip and peel it off.

Make the Dry Rub:
- In a small bowl, mix together smoked paprika, brown sugar, garlic powder, onion powder, salt, and black pepper to create the dry rub.

Season the Ribs:
- Rub the dry rub mixture all over the ribs, covering them evenly on both sides. Use your hands to press the rub into the meat.

Prepare the Smoker:
- Preheat your smoker to 225°F (110°C) using wood chips of your choice for smoking.

Smoke the Ribs:
- Place the seasoned ribs on the smoker grate, bone side down.
- Close the lid and smoke the ribs for about 3-4 hours, maintaining a steady temperature. Add more wood chips as needed to keep the smoke going.

Wrap the Ribs (Optional):
- After 3-4 hours, you can optionally wrap the ribs in aluminum foil to help tenderize them further. This step is known as the "Texas crutch."
- Place the ribs meat side down on a sheet of aluminum foil, drizzle with a little BBQ sauce, and wrap tightly. Return to the smoker and cook for another 1-2 hours, or until the ribs are tender.

Glaze with BBQ Sauce:
- About 30 minutes before the ribs are done, brush them with your favorite BBQ sauce.
- Continue cooking until the ribs are tender and the sauce has caramelized slightly.

Rest and Serve:

- Remove the ribs from the smoker and let them rest for 10-15 minutes before slicing.
- Slice the ribs between the bones and serve with extra BBQ sauce on the side.

Notes:

- Adjust the cooking time based on the thickness of your ribs and your desired level of tenderness.
- Feel free to experiment with different wood chips for smoking to achieve your preferred smoky flavor profile.
- Serve these delicious smoked paprika BBQ pork ribs as the main attraction at your beach BBQ or summer cookout. Enjoy the savory and smoky flavors!

Grilled Clams with White Wine and Garlic

Ingredients:

- 2 dozen fresh clams, scrubbed and cleaned
- 4 cloves garlic, minced
- 1/4 cup white wine
- 2 tablespoons olive oil
- Salt and pepper, to taste
- Chopped fresh parsley, for garnish
- Lemon wedges, for serving

Instructions:

Prepare the Clams:
- Rinse the clams under cold water and scrub them to remove any dirt or sand.
- Discard any clams that are open and do not close when tapped, as they may be dead and should not be eaten.

Make the Garlic White Wine Sauce:
- In a small bowl, combine the minced garlic, white wine, olive oil, salt, and pepper.

Grill the Clams:
- Preheat your grill to medium-high heat.
- Place the cleaned clams directly on the grill grates.
- Close the lid and grill the clams for about 5-7 minutes, or until they start to open.

Add the Sauce:
- Carefully remove the opened clams from the grill using tongs and transfer them to a large bowl.
- Pour the garlic white wine sauce over the grilled clams.

Serve:
- Toss the grilled clams gently to coat them with the sauce.
- Sprinkle with chopped fresh parsley for garnish.
- Serve the grilled clams hot with lemon wedges on the side for squeezing over the clams.

Notes:

- Make sure not to overcook the clams, as they can become tough and rubbery.
- Discard any clams that do not open after grilling, as they may be unsafe to eat.
- This grilled clams recipe is perfect as an appetizer or part of a seafood feast at your beach BBQ or outdoor gathering. Enjoy the delicious flavors of white wine and garlic with tender, smoky clams!

Moroccan Spiced Grilled Lamb Chops

Ingredients:

- 8 lamb loin chops, about 1 inch thick
- 2 tablespoons olive oil
- 2 tablespoons lemon juice
- 2 cloves garlic, minced
- 1 teaspoon ground cumin
- 1 teaspoon ground coriander
- 1 teaspoon paprika
- 1/2 teaspoon ground cinnamon
- 1/2 teaspoon ground ginger
- 1/2 teaspoon salt
- 1/4 teaspoon black pepper
- Fresh cilantro or parsley, chopped (for garnish)
- Lemon wedges, for serving

Instructions:

Prepare the Marinade:
- In a bowl, whisk together olive oil, lemon juice, minced garlic, ground cumin, ground coriander, paprika, ground cinnamon, ground ginger, salt, and black pepper to create the marinade.

Marinate the Lamb Chops:
- Place the lamb chops in a shallow dish or resealable plastic bag.
- Pour the marinade over the lamb chops, turning to coat them evenly.
- Cover and refrigerate for at least 1 hour, or up to overnight, to let the flavors develop.

Preheat the Grill:
- Preheat your grill to medium-high heat.

Grill the Lamb Chops:
- Remove the lamb chops from the marinade, allowing any excess marinade to drip off.
- Place the lamb chops on the preheated grill.
- Grill the lamb chops for about 3-4 minutes per side, or until they reach your desired level of doneness (medium-rare to medium).

Rest and Serve:
- Remove the grilled lamb chops from the grill and let them rest for a few minutes before serving.
- Sprinkle with chopped fresh cilantro or parsley for garnish.
- Serve the Moroccan spiced grilled lamb chops hot, accompanied by lemon wedges for squeezing over the chops.

Notes:

- Adjust the grilling time based on the thickness of your lamb chops and your preferred level of doneness.
- You can serve these flavorful lamb chops with couscous, rice, or grilled vegetables for a complete meal.
- This Moroccan spiced grilled lamb chops recipe is perfect for a special dinner or outdoor gathering. Enjoy the aromatic spices and tender, juicy lamb!

Grilled Watermelon and Feta Salad

Ingredients:

- 1 small seedless watermelon, sliced into wedges
- 1 tablespoon olive oil
- Salt and pepper, to taste
- 4 ounces feta cheese, crumbled
- 1/4 cup fresh mint leaves, chopped
- Balsamic glaze, for drizzling (optional)

Instructions:

Preheat the Grill:
- Preheat your grill to medium-high heat.

Grill the Watermelon:
- Brush the watermelon wedges with olive oil on both sides.
- Sprinkle with a little salt and pepper.
- Place the watermelon wedges directly on the preheated grill.
- Grill for about 2-3 minutes per side, or until grill marks appear and the watermelon is slightly caramelized.

Assemble the Salad:
- Remove the grilled watermelon from the grill and let it cool slightly.
- Cut the grilled watermelon into bite-sized pieces or cubes.
- In a large bowl, combine the grilled watermelon pieces with crumbled feta cheese and chopped fresh mint leaves.

Serve:
- Transfer the grilled watermelon and feta mixture to a serving platter or individual plates.
- Drizzle with balsamic glaze, if desired, for a touch of sweetness and acidity.
- Serve the grilled watermelon and feta salad immediately as a refreshing and unique summer dish.

Notes:

- You can customize this salad by adding additional ingredients such as arugula, thinly sliced red onions, or a squeeze of lime juice.
- Make sure to use ripe and sweet watermelon for the best flavor.
- The combination of sweet, smoky grilled watermelon with creamy feta cheese and fresh mint creates a delightful contrast of flavors and textures.
- Enjoy this grilled watermelon and feta salad as a side dish or appetizer at your next beach BBQ or outdoor gathering!

Korean BBQ Beef Bulgogi

Ingredients:

- 1.5 pounds beef sirloin or ribeye, thinly sliced
- 1/2 cup soy sauce
- 1/4 cup brown sugar
- 3 tablespoons sesame oil
- 4 cloves garlic, minced
- 1 small onion, grated
- 1 pear, grated (or substitute with apple)
- 2 tablespoons rice wine (mirin) or dry white wine
- 1 tablespoon grated ginger
- 2 green onions, chopped (for garnish)
- Toasted sesame seeds (for garnish)
- Optional: Sliced mushrooms, bell peppers, or onions

Instructions:

Prepare the Marinade:
- In a bowl, whisk together soy sauce, brown sugar, sesame oil, minced garlic, grated onion, grated pear (or apple), rice wine (or white wine), and grated ginger to make the marinade.

Marinate the Beef:
- Place the thinly sliced beef in a shallow dish or resealable plastic bag.
- Pour the marinade over the beef, making sure all pieces are well coated.
- Cover and refrigerate for at least 2 hours, or ideally overnight, to allow the flavors to penetrate the meat.

Grill the Bulgogi:
- Preheat your grill to medium-high heat.
- Remove the marinated beef from the refrigerator and let it come to room temperature.
- If using additional vegetables like mushrooms, bell peppers, or onions, you can skewer them separately for grilling.

Grill the Beef:
- Place the marinated beef slices directly on the preheated grill.
- Grill for about 2-3 minutes per side, or until the beef is cooked to your desired level of doneness and caramelized with grill marks.
- If using vegetables, grill them alongside the beef until tender.

Serve:
- Transfer the grilled beef bulgogi to a serving platter.
- Garnish with chopped green onions and toasted sesame seeds.

- Serve hot with steamed rice or wrapped in lettuce leaves (ssam), along with ssamjang (Korean dipping sauce) and any grilled vegetables.

Notes:

- You can also cook the beef bulgogi in a skillet or on a stovetop griddle if you prefer.
- Adjust the sweetness of the marinade by adding more or less brown sugar, according to your taste.
- Bulgogi is traditionally served with various banchan (side dishes) and condiments, so feel free to serve it with kimchi, pickled vegetables, and other Korean accompaniments.
- Enjoy this delicious and savory Korean BBQ beef bulgogi at your next outdoor gathering or barbecue!

Korean BBQ Beef Bulgogi

Ingredients:

- 1.5 pounds beef sirloin or ribeye, thinly sliced
- 1/2 cup soy sauce
- 1/4 cup brown sugar
- 3 tablespoons sesame oil
- 4 cloves garlic, minced
- 1 small onion, grated
- 1 pear, grated (or substitute with apple)
- 2 tablespoons rice wine (mirin) or dry white wine
- 1 tablespoon grated ginger
- 2 green onions, chopped (for garnish)
- Toasted sesame seeds (for garnish)
- Optional: Sliced mushrooms, bell peppers, or onions

Instructions:

Prepare the Marinade:
- In a bowl, combine soy sauce, brown sugar, sesame oil, minced garlic, grated onion, grated pear (or apple), rice wine (or white wine), and grated ginger. Whisk until the sugar is dissolved and the marinade is well combined.

Marinate the Beef:
- Place the thinly sliced beef in a large bowl or resealable plastic bag.
- Pour the marinade over the beef, making sure all pieces are coated evenly.
- Cover the bowl or seal the bag, and refrigerate for at least 2 hours, or preferably overnight, to allow the flavors to infuse into the meat.

Preheat the Grill:
- Preheat your grill to medium-high heat.

Grill the Bulgogi:
- Remove the marinated beef from the refrigerator and let it come to room temperature.
- If using any optional vegetables like mushrooms, bell peppers, or onions, skewer them separately for grilling.

Grill the Beef:
- Place the marinated beef slices directly on the preheated grill.

- Grill for about 2-3 minutes per side, or until the beef is cooked through and has a nice char from the grill.
- If grilling vegetables, cook them until tender and slightly charred.

Serve:
- Transfer the grilled beef bulgogi to a serving platter.
- Garnish with chopped green onions and toasted sesame seeds.
- Serve hot with steamed rice, lettuce leaves for wrapping (ssam), and Korean dipping sauces like ssamjang or gochujang.

Notes:

- Thinly sliced beef works best for bulgogi to ensure quick and even cooking on the grill.
- You can adjust the sweetness of the marinade by adding more or less brown sugar to suit your taste preferences.
- Feel free to customize your bulgogi by adding your favorite vegetables to the grill alongside the beef.
- Enjoy this delicious and flavorful Korean BBQ beef bulgogi at your next outdoor barbecue or gathering!

BBQ Chicken and Pineapple Pizza

Ingredients:

- 1 pound pizza dough (store-bought or homemade)
- 1 cup cooked and shredded chicken breast
- 1/2 cup BBQ sauce (your favorite variety)
- 1 cup diced pineapple (fresh or canned)
- 1 small red onion, thinly sliced
- 1 cup shredded mozzarella cheese
- Fresh cilantro, chopped (for garnish)
- Olive oil, for brushing

Instructions:

Preheat the Oven:
- Preheat your oven to the highest temperature setting (usually around 475-500°F or as high as your oven allows).

Prepare the Pizza Dough:
- On a lightly floured surface, roll out the pizza dough into your desired shape (round, rectangular, etc.) to fit your pizza stone or baking sheet.

Assemble the Pizza:
- Transfer the rolled-out pizza dough to a pizza stone or baking sheet lined with parchment paper.
- Brush the surface of the dough with a little olive oil.

Add Toppings:
- Spread BBQ sauce evenly over the oiled pizza dough, leaving a small border around the edges for the crust.
- Sprinkle the shredded chicken evenly over the BBQ sauce.
- Scatter diced pineapple and thinly sliced red onion over the chicken.
- Sprinkle shredded mozzarella cheese evenly over the top of the pizza.

Bake the Pizza:
- Place the assembled pizza in the preheated oven.
- Bake for 12-15 minutes, or until the crust is golden brown and the cheese is bubbly and melted.

Garnish and Serve:
- Remove the pizza from the oven and let it cool slightly.
- Sprinkle chopped fresh cilantro over the hot pizza for garnish.
- Slice the BBQ chicken and pineapple pizza into pieces and serve immediately.

Notes:

- Feel free to customize this pizza with additional toppings such as sliced bell peppers, cooked bacon, or jalapeño slices for a spicy kick.
- If using canned pineapple, make sure to drain it well before adding to the pizza.
- You can grill the chicken breast before shredding for added smoky flavor.
- Enjoy this BBQ chicken and pineapple pizza as a delicious and satisfying meal for a casual dinner or gathering with friends and family!

Grilled Lobster Mac and Cheese

Ingredients:

- 2 lobster tails, cooked and meat removed (about 8 ounces total)
- 8 ounces elbow macaroni or pasta of your choice
- 3 tablespoons butter
- 3 tablespoons all-purpose flour
- 2 cups milk (whole milk or half-and-half)
- 2 cups shredded sharp cheddar cheese
- 1 cup shredded Gruyere cheese (or substitute with more cheddar)
- Salt and pepper, to taste
- 1/4 teaspoon cayenne pepper (optional)
- 1/2 cup breadcrumbs (for topping)
- 2 tablespoons chopped fresh parsley (for garnish)
- Olive oil, for grilling

Instructions:

Prepare the Lobster:
- Cook the lobster tails by boiling them in salted water for about 8-10 minutes until the shells turn red and the meat is opaque. Remove the meat from the shells, chop into bite-sized pieces, and set aside.

Cook the Pasta:
- Cook the elbow macaroni or pasta according to the package instructions until al dente. Drain and set aside.

Make the Cheese Sauce:
- In a large saucepan, melt the butter over medium heat.
- Whisk in the flour to make a roux and cook for 1-2 minutes, stirring constantly.
- Gradually pour in the milk while whisking continuously to avoid lumps.
- Cook the sauce until thickened, about 5-7 minutes, stirring frequently.
- Reduce the heat to low and stir in the shredded cheddar cheese and Gruyere cheese until melted and smooth.
- Season the cheese sauce with salt, pepper, and cayenne pepper (if using).

Combine Pasta and Lobster:
- Preheat your grill to medium-high heat.
- In a large mixing bowl, combine the cooked pasta, chopped lobster meat, and cheese sauce. Mix until well coated.

Grill the Mac and Cheese:
- Brush a grill-safe baking dish or cast iron skillet with olive oil.
- Transfer the mac and cheese mixture into the greased dish, spreading it out evenly.
- Sprinkle breadcrumbs over the top of the mac and cheese for a crispy topping.

Grill-Bake the Mac and Cheese:
- Place the baking dish or skillet on the preheated grill.
- Close the grill lid and bake the lobster mac and cheese for about 15-20 minutes, or until the top is golden brown and the cheese is bubbly.

Serve:
- Remove the grilled lobster mac and cheese from the grill.
- Sprinkle chopped fresh parsley over the top for garnish.
- Let it cool slightly before serving.
- Enjoy this decadent grilled lobster mac and cheese as a main dish or side at your next outdoor gathering or special occasion!

Notes:

- You can add additional seasonings or ingredients to the cheese sauce, such as garlic powder, onion powder, or mustard for extra flavor.
- For a smoky flavor, you can use smoked cheddar cheese or add a dash of liquid smoke to the cheese sauce.
- Feel free to customize the toppings with crispy bacon bits or diced green onions for added texture and flavor.
- This grilled lobster mac and cheese is a rich and indulgent dish that's perfect for impressing guests or treating yourself to a gourmet outdoor meal!

Chili Lime Grilled Zucchini

Ingredients:

- 2 medium zucchini, sliced into long strips or rounds
- 2 tablespoons olive oil
- Zest and juice of 1 lime
- 1 teaspoon chili powder
- 1/2 teaspoon cumin
- 1/2 teaspoon garlic powder
- Salt and pepper, to taste
- Chopped fresh cilantro or parsley, for garnish (optional)

Instructions:

Preheat the Grill:
- Preheat your grill to medium-high heat.

Prepare the Zucchini:
- Wash the zucchini and slice them into long strips or rounds, about 1/4 inch thick.

Make the Marinade:
- In a small bowl, whisk together olive oil, lime zest, lime juice, chili powder, cumin, garlic powder, salt, and pepper to create the marinade.

Marinate the Zucchini:
- Place the zucchini slices in a shallow dish or resealable plastic bag.
- Pour the marinade over the zucchini, tossing to coat evenly.
- Let the zucchini marinate for at least 15-20 minutes to absorb the flavors.

Grill the Zucchini:
- Remove the zucchini slices from the marinade, shaking off any excess marinade.
- Place the zucchini slices directly on the preheated grill.
- Grill for about 3-4 minutes per side, or until the zucchini is tender and has nice grill marks.

Serve:
- Remove the grilled zucchini from the grill and transfer to a serving platter.
- Sprinkle with chopped fresh cilantro or parsley for garnish, if desired.
- Serve the chili lime grilled zucchini as a delicious side dish or appetizer.

Notes:

- Feel free to adjust the amount of chili powder and lime juice according to your preference for spice and tanginess.
- You can also add a pinch of red pepper flakes for extra heat.
- Grilled zucchini pairs well with grilled meats, seafood, or as part of a vegetarian meal.

- Enjoy this flavorful and zesty chili lime grilled zucchini at your next barbecue or outdoor gathering!

Honey Sriracha BBQ Wings

Ingredients:

- 2 pounds chicken wings, split into flats and drumettes
- Salt and pepper, to taste
- 1/2 cup BBQ sauce (your favorite variety)
- 3 tablespoons honey
- 2 tablespoons Sriracha sauce (adjust to taste)
- 2 tablespoons soy sauce
- 2 tablespoons butter
- 2 cloves garlic, minced
- 1 tablespoon lime juice
- Chopped green onions or cilantro, for garnish (optional)
- Sesame seeds, for garnish (optional)

Instructions:

Preheat the Oven:
- Preheat your oven to 425°F (220°C).

Prepare the Chicken Wings:
- Pat the chicken wings dry with paper towels.
- Season with salt and pepper to taste.

Bake the Chicken Wings:
- Arrange the seasoned chicken wings on a baking sheet lined with parchment paper.
- Bake in the preheated oven for 35-40 minutes, turning halfway through, until the wings are golden brown and crispy.

Make the Honey Sriracha BBQ Sauce:
- In a saucepan over medium heat, combine BBQ sauce, honey, Sriracha sauce, soy sauce, butter, minced garlic, and lime juice.
- Stir and cook until the sauce is heated through and the butter is melted. Taste and adjust the sweetness or spiciness to your liking.

Coat the Wings with Sauce:
- Remove the baked chicken wings from the oven.
- Place the wings in a large bowl and pour the honey Sriracha BBQ sauce over them.
- Toss the wings gently to coat them evenly with the sauce.

Return to Oven (Optional):
- If desired, return the sauced wings to the oven for an additional 5-7 minutes to caramelize the sauce slightly.

Serve:
- Transfer the honey Sriracha BBQ wings to a serving platter.

- Garnish with chopped green onions or cilantro and sesame seeds, if desired.
- Serve the wings hot as a delicious appetizer or main dish.

Notes:

- Adjust the amount of Sriracha sauce based on your spice preference. Add more for extra heat or less for a milder flavor.
- For a smokier flavor, you can use smoked BBQ sauce.
- Serve these honey Sriracha BBQ wings with ranch or blue cheese dressing and celery sticks for dipping.
- Enjoy these sticky, sweet, and spicy wings at your next party, game night, or family dinner!

Grilled Caesar Chicken Sandwiches

Ingredients:

- 4 boneless, skinless chicken breasts
- Salt and pepper, to taste
- 1 tablespoon olive oil
- 4 ciabatta rolls or sandwich buns
- Romaine lettuce leaves
- Shaved Parmesan cheese, for topping
- Caesar dressing (store-bought or homemade)

For Caesar Dressing:

- 1/2 cup mayonnaise
- 2 tablespoons grated Parmesan cheese
- 1 tablespoon fresh lemon juice
- 1 teaspoon Dijon mustard
- 1 garlic clove, minced
- Salt and pepper, to taste

Instructions:

Prepare the Chicken:
- Preheat your grill to medium-high heat.
- Season the chicken breasts with salt, pepper, and olive oil.

Grill the Chicken:
- Place the seasoned chicken breasts on the preheated grill.
- Grill for about 6-8 minutes per side, or until the chicken is fully cooked (internal temperature of 165°F or 74°C).
- Remove from the grill and let the chicken rest for a few minutes before slicing.

Make the Caesar Dressing:
- In a bowl, whisk together mayonnaise, grated Parmesan cheese, fresh lemon juice, Dijon mustard, minced garlic, salt, and pepper until well combined.
- Adjust the seasoning to taste. Add a little water to thin out the dressing if desired.

Assemble the Sandwiches:

- Slice the ciabatta rolls or sandwich buns in half.
- Spread a generous amount of Caesar dressing on the bottom halves of the rolls.
- Layer with romaine lettuce leaves.
- Place a grilled chicken breast on top of the lettuce.

Add Toppings:
- Drizzle more Caesar dressing over the grilled chicken.
- Top with shaved Parmesan cheese.

Serve:
- Close the sandwiches with the top halves of the rolls.
- Serve the grilled Caesar chicken sandwiches immediately.

Notes:

- You can use store-bought Caesar dressing to save time, or make your own using the recipe provided.
- Feel free to add other toppings like crispy bacon, sliced tomatoes, or avocado slices to customize your sandwiches.
- Serve these delicious grilled Caesar chicken sandwiches with a side of potato chips, fries, or a simple green salad.
- Enjoy these flavorful sandwiches for lunch, dinner, or a picnic with family and friends!

Bourbon BBQ Glazed Pork Belly

Ingredients:

- 2 pounds pork belly, skin removed and cut into cubes or slices
- Salt and pepper, to taste
- 1/2 cup bourbon
- 1/2 cup BBQ sauce (your favorite variety)
- 1/4 cup brown sugar
- 2 tablespoons soy sauce
- 2 tablespoons apple cider vinegar
- 2 cloves garlic, minced
- 1 teaspoon smoked paprika
- 1/2 teaspoon ground cumin
- 1/2 teaspoon chili powder
- Chopped fresh parsley or green onions, for garnish (optional)

Instructions:

Preheat the Oven:
- Preheat your oven to 325°F (160°C).

Prepare the Pork Belly:
- Season the pork belly pieces with salt and pepper.

Sear the Pork Belly (Optional):
- Heat a large oven-safe skillet or Dutch oven over medium-high heat.
- Add the pork belly pieces and sear on all sides until golden brown and crispy. This step adds extra flavor, but you can skip it if preferred.

Make the Bourbon BBQ Glaze:
- In a bowl, whisk together bourbon, BBQ sauce, brown sugar, soy sauce, apple cider vinegar, minced garlic, smoked paprika, ground cumin, and chili powder to make the glaze.

Combine and Braise:
- Place the seared or raw pork belly pieces in a single layer in the skillet or Dutch oven.
- Pour the bourbon BBQ glaze over the pork belly, making sure each piece is coated.

Bake the Pork Belly:
- Cover the skillet or Dutch oven with a lid or foil.

- Transfer to the preheated oven and bake for 2 to 2 1/2 hours, or until the pork belly is tender and caramelized, basting with the glaze halfway through cooking.

Serve:
- Remove the pork belly from the oven.
- Transfer the pork belly pieces to a serving platter or dish.
- Spoon any remaining glaze from the skillet or Dutch oven over the pork belly.
- Garnish with chopped fresh parsley or green onions, if desired.
- Serve the bourbon BBQ glazed pork belly hot as a main dish or appetizer.

Notes:

- You can adjust the sweetness or spiciness of the glaze by varying the amount of brown sugar or chili powder.
- For a smokier flavor, you can add a dash of liquid smoke to the bourbon BBQ glaze.
- Serve this delicious bourbon BBQ glazed pork belly with coleslaw, mashed potatoes, or grilled vegetables for a complete meal.
- Enjoy the rich flavors of bourbon and BBQ in this mouthwatering pork belly dish!

Mediterranean Grilled Swordfish

Ingredients:

- 4 swordfish steaks, about 6 ounces each
- Salt and pepper, to taste
- 2 tablespoons olive oil
- 2 cloves garlic, minced
- 1 teaspoon dried oregano
- 1 teaspoon dried thyme
- Zest and juice of 1 lemon
- 1/4 cup chopped fresh parsley
- Lemon wedges, for serving

Instructions:

Prepare the Swordfish:
- Pat the swordfish steaks dry with paper towels.
- Season both sides of the swordfish steaks with salt and pepper.

Make the Marinade:
- In a bowl, whisk together olive oil, minced garlic, dried oregano, dried thyme, lemon zest, and lemon juice to create the marinade.

Marinate the Swordfish:
- Place the swordfish steaks in a shallow dish or resealable plastic bag.
- Pour the marinade over the swordfish, turning to coat evenly.
- Cover and refrigerate for at least 30 minutes to 1 hour, allowing the flavors to meld.

Preheat the Grill:
- Preheat your grill to medium-high heat.

Grill the Swordfish:
- Remove the swordfish steaks from the marinade, shaking off any excess marinade.
- Place the swordfish steaks directly on the preheated grill.
- Grill for about 4-5 minutes per side, or until the swordfish is cooked through and has nice grill marks. The internal temperature should reach 145°F (63°C).

Serve:
- Remove the grilled swordfish from the grill and transfer to a serving platter.
- Sprinkle chopped fresh parsley over the grilled swordfish.
- Serve hot with lemon wedges on the side for squeezing over the fish.

Notes:

- Ensure your grill grates are clean and well-oiled to prevent the swordfish from sticking.
- Swordfish is a firm fish and holds up well on the grill. Avoid overcooking to prevent the fish from becoming dry.
- This Mediterranean grilled swordfish pairs well with couscous, rice, or a fresh salad.
- Enjoy the delicious flavors of garlic, herbs, and lemon in this simple and flavorful grilled swordfish recipe!

Hawaiian BBQ Pork Sliders

Ingredients:

- 1 pound pork shoulder or pork butt, trimmed and cut into chunks
- Salt and pepper, to taste
- 1 cup BBQ sauce (your favorite variety)
- 1/2 cup pineapple juice
- 1/4 cup soy sauce
- 2 cloves garlic, minced
- 1 tablespoon brown sugar
- Slider buns
- Pineapple slices, for serving
- Coleslaw, for serving (optional)
- Sliced jalapeños, for serving (optional)

Instructions:

Prepare the Pork:
- Season the pork chunks with salt and pepper.

Make the BBQ Sauce:
- In a bowl, whisk together BBQ sauce, pineapple juice, soy sauce, minced garlic, and brown sugar to create the BBQ sauce.

Cook the Pork:
- Place the seasoned pork chunks in a slow cooker or Instant Pot.
- Pour the BBQ sauce mixture over the pork, ensuring all pieces are coated.

Slow Cooker Method:
- Cover and cook on low for 6-8 hours or on high for 3-4 hours, until the pork is tender and easily shreds with a fork.

Instant Pot Method:
- Close the lid and set the Instant Pot to "Manual" or "Pressure Cook" mode for 60 minutes.
- Allow natural pressure release for 10 minutes before quick releasing any remaining pressure.

Shred the Pork:
- Once the pork is cooked and tender, use two forks to shred the meat directly in the slow cooker or Instant Pot, mixing it with the sauce.

Assemble the Sliders:
- Toast the slider buns lightly, if desired.
- Place a generous amount of BBQ pulled pork onto each slider bun.
- Top with a pineapple slice and coleslaw, if using.
- Optionally, add sliced jalapeños for a spicy kick.

Serve:

- Arrange the Hawaiian BBQ pork sliders on a platter.
- Serve immediately and enjoy these delicious sliders as a party appetizer or main dish.

Notes:

- You can customize the level of sweetness and spiciness in the BBQ sauce by adjusting the amount of brown sugar or adding more or less soy sauce and garlic.
- Leftover Hawaiian BBQ pulled pork can be stored in the refrigerator for a few days and used in sandwiches, wraps, or rice bowls.
- These sliders are perfect for gatherings, potlucks, or game day parties. Enjoy the tropical flavors of pineapple and BBQ in every bite!

Grilled Portobello Mushrooms with Balsamic Glaze

Ingredients:

- 4 large portobello mushrooms, stems removed
- 3 tablespoons balsamic vinegar
- 2 tablespoons olive oil
- 2 cloves garlic, minced
- Salt and pepper, to taste
- Fresh chopped parsley or basil, for garnish (optional)

Instructions:

Prepare the Portobello Mushrooms:
- Clean the portobello mushrooms by gently wiping them with a damp paper towel to remove any dirt.
- Remove the stems by twisting them off or cutting them with a knife.

Make the Marinade:
- In a small bowl, whisk together balsamic vinegar, olive oil, minced garlic, salt, and pepper to create the marinade.

Marinate the Mushrooms:
- Place the portobello mushrooms in a shallow dish or resealable plastic bag.
- Pour the marinade over the mushrooms, turning to coat evenly.
- Allow the mushrooms to marinate for at least 30 minutes, turning occasionally.

Preheat the Grill:
- Preheat your grill to medium-high heat.

Grill the Portobello Mushrooms:
- Remove the mushrooms from the marinade, reserving any excess marinade for basting.
- Place the mushrooms on the preheated grill, gill side down.
- Grill for about 4-5 minutes per side, or until the mushrooms are tender and have nice grill marks.

Baste with Marinade (Optional):
- While grilling, you can baste the mushrooms with the reserved marinade for extra flavor.

Serve:
- Transfer the grilled portobello mushrooms to a serving platter.

- Garnish with fresh chopped parsley or basil, if desired.
- Serve the grilled portobello mushrooms as a side dish or appetizer.

Notes:

- You can add additional herbs or spices to the marinade, such as dried thyme or rosemary, for extra flavor.
- Serve these grilled portobello mushrooms on their own or as a topping for burgers, salads, or pasta dishes.
- Enjoy the rich and savory flavors of these grilled portobello mushrooms with a drizzle of balsamic glaze for a delightful vegetarian dish!

Chipotle BBQ Sweet Potato Wedges

Ingredients:

- 2 large sweet potatoes, scrubbed and cut into wedges
- 2 tablespoons olive oil
- 1 tablespoon chipotle chili powder
- 1 teaspoon smoked paprika
- 1 teaspoon garlic powder
- 1/2 teaspoon onion powder
- Salt and pepper, to taste
- 1/4 cup BBQ sauce (your favorite variety)
- Chopped fresh cilantro or parsley, for garnish (optional)

Instructions:

Preheat the Oven:
- Preheat your oven to 425°F (220°C) and line a baking sheet with parchment paper or aluminum foil.

Prepare the Sweet Potato Wedges:
- Scrub the sweet potatoes clean and cut them lengthwise into wedges.

Season the Sweet Potatoes:
- In a large bowl, toss the sweet potato wedges with olive oil, chipotle chili powder, smoked paprika, garlic powder, onion powder, salt, and pepper. Make sure the wedges are evenly coated with the seasonings.

Bake the Sweet Potato Wedges:
- Arrange the seasoned sweet potato wedges in a single layer on the prepared baking sheet.
- Bake in the preheated oven for 25-30 minutes, flipping halfway through, until the wedges are tender and caramelized.

Coat with BBQ Sauce:
- Remove the baked sweet potato wedges from the oven.
- Brush the wedges with BBQ sauce, coating them evenly on all sides.

Return to Oven:
- Return the BBQ-coated sweet potato wedges to the oven and bake for an additional 5-7 minutes, or until the BBQ sauce is slightly caramelized.

Serve:
- Transfer the chipotle BBQ sweet potato wedges to a serving platter.
- Garnish with chopped fresh cilantro or parsley, if desired.
- Serve hot as a delicious side dish or snack.

Notes:

- Adjust the amount of chipotle chili powder based on your spice preference. Add more for extra heat or less for a milder flavor.
- Feel free to use your favorite BBQ sauce for coating the sweet potato wedges. Choose a smoky or sweet BBQ sauce depending on your taste.
- These chipotle BBQ sweet potato wedges are perfect for serving as a side dish with grilled meats, burgers, or sandwiches. Enjoy their sweet and spicy flavor!

Tangy Mango BBQ Pulled Pork

Ingredients:

- 3-4 pounds pork shoulder or pork butt, trimmed of excess fat
- Salt and pepper, to taste
- 1 tablespoon olive oil
- 1 onion, diced
- 3 cloves garlic, minced
- 2 cups diced ripe mango (fresh or frozen)
- 1 cup ketchup
- 1/2 cup apple cider vinegar
- 1/4 cup brown sugar
- 2 tablespoons Dijon mustard
- 1 tablespoon Worcestershire sauce
- 1 teaspoon chili powder
- 1/2 teaspoon smoked paprika
- Hamburger buns or sandwich rolls, for serving
- Coleslaw, for topping (optional)

Instructions:

Prepare the Pork:
- Season the pork shoulder or pork butt generously with salt and pepper.

Sear the Pork:
- Heat olive oil in a large skillet or Dutch oven over medium-high heat.
- Sear the seasoned pork on all sides until browned. This adds flavor and helps seal in juices.

Make the Mango BBQ Sauce:
- In the same skillet or Dutch oven, add diced onion and minced garlic. Sauté until softened and fragrant.
- Add diced mango, ketchup, apple cider vinegar, brown sugar, Dijon mustard, Worcestershire sauce, chili powder, and smoked paprika to the skillet. Stir to combine.

Cook the Pork:
- Return the seared pork to the skillet, nestling it into the mango BBQ sauce.
- Cover the skillet or Dutch oven with a lid and reduce the heat to low.

- Simmer for 3-4 hours, or until the pork is tender and easily shreds with a fork. Alternatively, transfer the skillet or Dutch oven to a preheated 325°F (160°C) oven and braise for 3-4 hours.

Shred the Pork:
- Once the pork is tender, use two forks to shred the meat directly in the skillet or Dutch oven, mixing it with the mango BBQ sauce.

Serve:
- Serve the tangy mango BBQ pulled pork on hamburger buns or sandwich rolls.
- Top with coleslaw for a delicious contrast in textures and flavors.

Notes:

- If fresh mangoes are not available, you can use frozen diced mango. Ensure they are thawed before using.
- Adjust the sweetness or tanginess of the BBQ sauce by varying the amount of brown sugar or apple cider vinegar.
- Leftover mango BBQ pulled pork can be refrigerated for a few days or frozen for longer storage. Enjoy it in sandwiches, tacos, quesadillas, or on top of salads!
- This tangy mango BBQ pulled pork is perfect for summer gatherings, potlucks, or weeknight dinners. Enjoy the tropical twist on a classic pulled pork dish!

Grilled Asparagus with Lemon Zest

Ingredients:

- 1 bunch of asparagus spears, woody ends trimmed
- 2 tablespoons olive oil
- Salt and pepper, to taste
- Zest of 1 lemon
- Lemon wedges, for serving (optional)

Instructions:

Preheat the Grill:
- Preheat your grill to medium-high heat.

Prepare the Asparagus:
- Trim the woody ends off the asparagus spears.

Season the Asparagus:
- In a large bowl, toss the asparagus spears with olive oil, salt, and pepper until evenly coated.

Grill the Asparagus:
- Place the seasoned asparagus spears directly on the preheated grill.
- Grill for 5-7 minutes, turning occasionally with tongs, until the asparagus is tender and slightly charred.

Finish with Lemon Zest:
- Remove the grilled asparagus from the grill and transfer to a serving platter.
- Sprinkle the lemon zest over the grilled asparagus while it's still hot to infuse the flavors.

Serve:
- Garnish with additional lemon wedges, if desired.
- Serve the grilled asparagus with lemon zest as a delicious side dish to complement grilled meats, seafood, or as part of a vegetarian meal.

Notes:

- Be sure not to overcook the asparagus to maintain its crisp texture.
- You can add other seasonings such as garlic powder, smoked paprika, or crushed red pepper flakes for extra flavor.

- Grilled asparagus with lemon zest is a simple and elegant dish that's perfect for spring and summer gatherings. Enjoy its bright and fresh flavors!

BBQ Jackfruit Sandwiches

Ingredients:

- 2 cans (20 ounces each) young green jackfruit in brine or water
- 1 tablespoon olive oil
- 1 onion, finely chopped
- 3 cloves garlic, minced
- 1 cup BBQ sauce (your favorite variety)
- 1/2 cup vegetable broth or water
- 1 tablespoon soy sauce or tamari
- 1 tablespoon maple syrup or brown sugar
- Salt and pepper, to taste
- Hamburger buns or sandwich rolls
- Coleslaw or pickles, for topping (optional)

Instructions:

Prepare the Jackfruit:
- Drain and rinse the canned jackfruit under cold water.
- Using your hands or a fork, shred the jackfruit into smaller pieces, discarding any hard cores or seeds.

Sauté the Onion and Garlic:
- In a large skillet or saucepan, heat olive oil over medium heat.
- Add chopped onion and minced garlic. Sauté until the onion is translucent and fragrant.

Cook the Jackfruit:
- Add the shredded jackfruit to the skillet with the sautéed onion and garlic.
- Stir in BBQ sauce, vegetable broth (or water), soy sauce (or tamari), maple syrup (or brown sugar), salt, and pepper.
- Mix well to combine all ingredients.

Simmer the BBQ Jackfruit:
- Bring the mixture to a simmer over medium-low heat.
- Cover and cook for 20-25 minutes, stirring occasionally, until the jackfruit is tender and absorbs the flavors of the BBQ sauce.

Assemble the Sandwiches:
- Toast the hamburger buns or sandwich rolls lightly, if desired.
- Spoon the BBQ jackfruit mixture onto the bottom halves of the buns.
- Top with coleslaw, pickles, or your favorite toppings.

Serve:
- Close the sandwiches with the top halves of the buns.
- Serve the BBQ jackfruit sandwiches hot and enjoy!

Notes:

- Young green jackfruit has a neutral taste and fibrous texture, making it a great vegan substitute for pulled pork.
- Adjust the sweetness and saltiness of the BBQ jackfruit filling to suit your taste preferences by varying the amount of maple syrup (or brown sugar) and soy sauce (or tamari).
- BBQ jackfruit sandwiches are a delicious plant-based alternative to pulled pork sandwiches. They're perfect for vegan or vegetarian meals and are sure to satisfy everyone at your table!

Coconut Lime Grilled Sweet Potatoes

Ingredients:

- 2 large sweet potatoes, peeled and sliced into rounds or wedges
- 1/4 cup coconut milk
- Zest and juice of 1 lime
- 2 tablespoons olive oil
- 1 tablespoon honey or maple syrup (optional)
- Salt and pepper, to taste
- Fresh chopped cilantro or parsley, for garnish (optional)

Instructions:

Preheat the Grill:
- Preheat your grill to medium-high heat.

Prepare the Sweet Potatoes:
- Peel the sweet potatoes and slice them into rounds or wedges, about 1/4 to 1/2 inch thick.

Make the Marinade:
- In a bowl, whisk together coconut milk, lime zest, lime juice, olive oil, honey or maple syrup (if using), salt, and pepper to create the marinade.

Marinate the Sweet Potatoes:
- Place the sweet potato slices in a shallow dish or resealable plastic bag.
- Pour the marinade over the sweet potatoes, turning to coat evenly.
- Let the sweet potatoes marinate for at least 30 minutes to 1 hour, allowing the flavors to meld.

Grill the Sweet Potatoes:
- Remove the sweet potato slices from the marinade, reserving any excess marinade for basting.
- Place the sweet potato slices directly on the preheated grill.
- Grill for about 4-5 minutes per side, or until the sweet potatoes are tender and have nice grill marks. Baste with the reserved marinade while grilling.

Serve:
- Remove the grilled sweet potatoes from the grill and transfer to a serving platter.
- Garnish with fresh chopped cilantro or parsley, if desired.
- Serve the coconut lime grilled sweet potatoes as a delicious side dish or appetizer.

Notes:

- Adjust the sweetness and tanginess of the marinade by varying the amount of honey or lime juice.
- You can add a pinch of chili powder or red pepper flakes to the marinade for a spicy kick.
- Grilled coconut lime sweet potatoes pair well with grilled meats, seafood, or as part of a vegetarian meal. Enjoy the tropical flavors!

Cajun Grilled Oysters

Ingredients:

- 12 fresh oysters, scrubbed and cleaned
- 1/2 cup unsalted butter, melted
- 2 cloves garlic, minced
- 1 tablespoon Cajun seasoning (store-bought or homemade)
- 1 tablespoon lemon juice
- Chopped fresh parsley, for garnish
- Lemon wedges, for serving

Instructions:

Preheat the Grill:
- Preheat your grill to medium-high heat.

Prepare the Oysters:
- Scrub the oysters under cold water to remove any dirt or debris.
- Use an oyster knife to carefully shuck the oysters, removing the top shell and loosening the oyster from the bottom shell. Leave the oysters in the bottom shell.

Make the Cajun Butter Sauce:
- In a small saucepan or microwave-safe bowl, melt the unsalted butter.
- Stir in minced garlic, Cajun seasoning, and lemon juice. Mix well to combine.

Grill the Oysters:
- Place the cleaned oysters directly on the preheated grill, flat side up.
- Spoon the Cajun butter sauce over each oyster, covering the entire surface.

Cook the Oysters:
- Close the grill lid and cook the oysters for about 5-7 minutes, or until the oyster edges start to curl and the butter is bubbling.

Serve:
- Carefully remove the grilled oysters from the grill using tongs or a spatula.
- Transfer the grilled oysters to a serving platter.
- Garnish with chopped fresh parsley and serve immediately with lemon wedges on the side.

Notes:

- Be cautious when shucking oysters and use a sturdy oyster knife to avoid injury.
- Adjust the amount of Cajun seasoning based on your spice preference. Add more for extra heat or less for a milder flavor.
- Serve these Cajun grilled oysters as a delicious appetizer or part of a seafood feast. Enjoy the bold flavors and savory taste of grilled oysters!

Caribbean BBQ Chicken Quesadillas

Ingredients:

- 2 boneless, skinless chicken breasts, cooked and shredded
- 1 cup Caribbean-style BBQ sauce (or regular BBQ sauce with added Caribbean spices like jerk seasoning)
- 4 large flour tortillas
- 2 cups shredded cheese (cheddar, Monterey Jack, or a blend)
- 1/2 red bell pepper, diced
- 1/2 red onion, diced
- 1/4 cup chopped fresh cilantro
- 2 tablespoons olive oil or butter, for cooking
- Sour cream, salsa, or guacamole, for serving (optional)

Instructions:

Prepare the BBQ Chicken:
- Cook the chicken breasts (boil, bake, or grill) until fully cooked and tender.
- Shred the cooked chicken using two forks.

Mix Chicken with BBQ Sauce:
- In a bowl, combine the shredded chicken with Caribbean-style BBQ sauce. Ensure the chicken is well coated with the sauce.

Assemble the Quesadillas:
- Place a flour tortilla on a clean work surface.
- Spread a layer of shredded cheese evenly over half of the tortilla.
- Spoon a portion of the BBQ chicken mixture over the cheese.
- Sprinkle diced red bell pepper, red onion, and chopped cilantro over the chicken.
- Top with another layer of shredded cheese.
- Fold the empty half of the tortilla over the filling to create a half-moon shape.

Cook the Quesadillas:
- Heat 1 tablespoon of olive oil or butter in a large skillet over medium heat.
- Carefully place the assembled quesadilla in the skillet and cook for 3-4 minutes, or until the bottom is golden brown and crispy.

Flip and Cook the Other Side:
- Carefully flip the quesadilla to cook the other side for an additional 3-4 minutes, or until golden brown and crispy.
- Press down lightly with a spatula to ensure the cheese is melted and the filling is heated through.

Repeat with Remaining Ingredients:
- Remove the cooked quesadilla from the skillet and repeat the process with the remaining tortillas and filling ingredients.
- You may need to add more olive oil or butter to the skillet between batches.

Serve and Enjoy:
- Cut the cooked quesadillas into wedges using a sharp knife or pizza cutter.
- Serve hot with sour cream, salsa, or guacamole on the side for dipping, if desired.

Notes:

- Feel free to customize the filling with additional ingredients such as sliced jalapeños, black beans, or corn kernels.
- Use a Caribbean-style BBQ sauce with flavors like jerk seasoning, mango, or pineapple for an authentic Caribbean taste.
- These Caribbean BBQ chicken quesadillas are perfect for a quick and flavorful meal. Enjoy the tropical flavors wrapped in crispy tortillas!

Grilled Eggplant Caprese Salad

Ingredients:

- 1 large eggplant, sliced into rounds (about 1/2 inch thick)
- 2 tablespoons olive oil
- Salt and pepper, to taste
- 1 pint cherry tomatoes, halved
- 8 ounces fresh mozzarella cheese, sliced
- Fresh basil leaves
- Balsamic glaze, for drizzling

Instructions:

Preheat the Grill:
- Preheat your grill to medium-high heat.

Prepare the Eggplant:
- Brush both sides of the eggplant slices with olive oil.
- Season with salt and pepper.

Grill the Eggplant:
- Place the eggplant slices on the preheated grill.
- Grill for about 3-4 minutes per side, or until tender and grill marks appear.
- Remove from the grill and set aside to cool slightly.

Assemble the Salad:
- On a serving platter, arrange the grilled eggplant slices.
- Top each slice with halved cherry tomatoes.

Add Mozzarella and Basil:
- Place a slice of fresh mozzarella on top of each eggplant slice.
- Top with fresh basil leaves.

Drizzle with Balsamic Glaze:
- Drizzle the assembled salad with balsamic glaze.

Serve:
- Serve the grilled eggplant Caprese salad immediately, while still warm, as a delicious appetizer or side dish.

Notes:

- You can add extra flavor by marinating the eggplant slices in a mixture of olive oil, garlic, and herbs before grilling.

- Feel free to sprinkle some freshly ground black pepper or red pepper flakes over the salad for a touch of spice.
- This grilled eggplant Caprese salad is a wonderful vegetarian dish that showcases the flavors of summer. Enjoy the combination of grilled eggplant, fresh tomatoes, creamy mozzarella, and aromatic basil!

Smoked Salmon Dip with Grilled Pita

Ingredients:

- 8 ounces smoked salmon, finely chopped
- 8 ounces cream cheese, softened
- 1/2 cup sour cream
- 2 tablespoons mayonnaise
- 1 tablespoon freshly squeezed lemon juice
- 2 green onions, finely chopped
- 1 tablespoon capers, drained and chopped
- 1 teaspoon Dijon mustard
- Salt and pepper, to taste
- Fresh dill, chopped (for garnish)
- Grilled pita bread or pita chips, for serving

Instructions:

Prepare the Smoked Salmon Dip:
- In a mixing bowl, combine the softened cream cheese, sour cream, mayonnaise, and Dijon mustard. Mix until smooth and well combined.

Add Flavorings:
- Stir in the chopped smoked salmon, green onions, capers, and freshly squeezed lemon juice into the cream cheese mixture.
- Season with salt and pepper to taste. Adjust seasoning as needed.

Chill the Dip:
- Cover the bowl with plastic wrap and refrigerate the smoked salmon dip for at least 1 hour to allow the flavors to meld together.

Grill the Pita Bread:
- Preheat a grill or grill pan over medium-high heat.
- Lightly brush both sides of the pita bread with olive oil.
- Grill the pita bread for about 1-2 minutes per side, or until lightly charred and crispy. Alternatively, you can toast the pita bread in a toaster or oven.

Serve:
- Transfer the chilled smoked salmon dip to a serving bowl.
- Garnish with chopped fresh dill.
- Serve the smoked salmon dip with grilled pita bread or pita chips on the side.

Notes:

- You can customize the texture of the smoked salmon dip by adjusting the amount of sour cream and mayonnaise. Add more for a creamier dip or less for a thicker consistency.
- Feel free to add additional herbs or spices like chopped parsley, chives, or a dash of hot sauce for extra flavor.
- This smoked salmon dip is perfect for parties, gatherings, or as an elegant appetizer. Enjoy the creamy and flavorful dip with crispy grilled pita bread!

Thai Chili Lime Grilled Beef Skewers

Ingredients:

- 1.5 lbs beef sirloin or flank steak, thinly sliced
- 1/4 cup soy sauce
- 2 tablespoons fish sauce
- 2 tablespoons fresh lime juice
- 2 tablespoons honey
- 2 tablespoons vegetable oil
- 3 cloves garlic, minced
- 2 tablespoons finely chopped lemongrass (white part only)
- 1-2 Thai bird's eye chilies, finely chopped (adjust to taste)
- 1 teaspoon ground coriander
- 1 teaspoon ground cumin
- 1/2 teaspoon turmeric powder
- Salt and pepper, to taste
- Bamboo skewers, soaked in water for 30 minutes

Instructions:

Prepare the Marinade:
- In a bowl, combine soy sauce, fish sauce, lime juice, honey, vegetable oil, minced garlic, chopped lemongrass, chopped Thai chilies, ground coriander, ground cumin, turmeric powder, salt, and pepper. Mix well.

Marinate the Beef:
- Place the thinly sliced beef in a shallow dish or resealable plastic bag.
- Pour the marinade over the beef, making sure it is evenly coated.
- Cover and refrigerate for at least 2 hours, or ideally overnight, to allow the flavors to infuse.

Skewer the Beef:
- Preheat your grill to medium-high heat.
- Thread the marinated beef slices onto bamboo skewers, folding the slices as needed to create even layers.

Grill the Skewers:
- Place the beef skewers on the preheated grill.
- Grill for about 3-4 minutes on each side, or until the beef is cooked to your desired doneness and has nice grill marks.

Serve:
- Remove the grilled beef skewers from the grill.
- Transfer to a serving platter and garnish with extra lime wedges and chopped cilantro, if desired.

- Serve immediately as an appetizer or main dish with steamed rice and your favorite dipping sauce.

Notes:

- Adjust the amount of Thai bird's eye chilies based on your spice preference. Use more chilies for a spicier flavor or reduce the amount for a milder taste.
- For best results, thinly slice the beef against the grain to ensure tenderness.
- These Thai chili lime grilled beef skewers are perfect for summer grilling and can be enjoyed with a side of cucumber salad or Thai sticky rice. Enjoy the flavorful and aromatic Thai-inspired dish!

BBQ Pineapple Upside-Down Cake

Ingredients:

For the Pineapple Topping:

- 1/2 cup (1 stick) unsalted butter
- 1 cup brown sugar, packed
- 1 can (20 ounces) pineapple slices (reserve the juice)
- Maraschino cherries, for garnish

For the Cake Batter:

- 1 1/2 cups all-purpose flour
- 1 1/2 teaspoons baking powder
- 1/4 teaspoon salt
- 1/2 cup unsalted butter, softened
- 1 cup granulated sugar
- 2 large eggs
- 1 teaspoon vanilla extract
- 1/2 cup pineapple juice (reserved from the canned pineapple)
- 1/4 cup milk

Instructions:

Prepare the Pineapple Topping:
- In a saucepan, melt the butter over medium heat.
- Add the brown sugar and stir until dissolved and bubbly.
- Pour the butter-sugar mixture into a 9-inch round cake pan, spreading it evenly.
- Arrange pineapple slices on top of the butter-sugar mixture. Place a maraschino cherry in the center of each pineapple slice.

Prepare the Cake Batter:
- In a medium bowl, whisk together the flour, baking powder, and salt. Set aside.
- In a large bowl, cream together the softened butter and granulated sugar until light and fluffy.
- Beat in the eggs, one at a time, and then add the vanilla extract.

Combine Wet and Dry Ingredients:
- Gradually add the flour mixture to the creamed mixture, alternating with the pineapple juice and milk. Begin and end with the flour mixture, mixing until just combined.

Assemble and Grill the Cake:
- Preheat your grill to 350°F (175°C) for indirect grilling.

- Carefully pour the cake batter over the pineapple slices in the cake pan, spreading it evenly.

Grill the Cake:
- Place the cake pan on the grill over indirect heat.
- Close the grill lid and bake the cake for 30-35 minutes, or until a toothpick inserted into the center comes out clean.

Cool and Invert the Cake:
- Remove the cake from the grill and let it cool in the pan for 10 minutes.
- Run a knife around the edges of the cake to loosen it from the pan.
- Place a serving plate upside down over the cake pan and carefully invert the cake onto the plate. Allow the pan to rest on top of the cake for a few minutes to let the caramelized topping drip down.

Serve:
- Lift off the cake pan and reveal the beautiful BBQ pineapple upside-down cake.
- Slice and serve the cake warm or at room temperature. Enjoy!

Notes:

- Ensure that your grill is preheated to the correct temperature and set up for indirect heat to avoid burning the cake.
- You can customize this recipe by adding chopped macadamia nuts or shredded coconut to the cake batter for extra texture and flavor.
- This BBQ pineapple upside-down cake is a delightful dessert that captures the tropical flavors of pineapple and is perfect for outdoor grilling gatherings. Enjoy the sweet and caramelized goodness!